MW01235781

All references unless otherwise noted are taken from
the NIV Worship (2000)

TransFit Athens
1225 S. Milledge Avenue
Athens, GA 30605

www.transfitathens.com

"Do not conform to
the patterns of this
world but be
transformed by the
renewing of your
mind"

Romans 12:2

Table of Contents

Introduction and Letter

Welcome

Hello sweet friend! I am so excited to start this journey with you. When you think of the word "transformation," what immediately pops into your mind? Is it the possibility of a different looking body? A renewed spirit and joyful heart? Or a transformed life in which you are satisfied and content with just being you? Is it okay to have these racing thoughts?

Of course! I have crazy thoughts constantly, but beneath many layers, I truly yearn to have a deeper transformation- a total body, mind and spirit transformation; a complete healing in the deepest part of my soul.

My prayer for you is that in the next six weeks we spend together, you will not only make a transformation in your health and fitness, but you can transform your entire life. But why? Why should you commit to following through with the Live Transformed study? Because you yearn for something more, something you can hold on to for life. Your transformation journey is not a fad diet or hottest workout trend but a plan that will last. The time is NOW to take action! Let's make ourselves ready to work and serve for His glory. We have been given this beautiful, amazing gift of a body and our Father wants us to use this gift to produce good works. By glorifying God in our bodies with what we eat, what we drink, and how we act, we can serve, love, and live life to the fullest. Allow the Holy Spirit to move through your entire being over the next six weeks. I will be with you in spirit throughout your journey, and I will be praying for you to be transformed by God's love for you!

Blessings, Caroline

How To use this Study

The Live Transformed study is meant to be an interactive exchange between you and the One who created you, your Heavenly Father. Each day, I encourage you to take time to pray, meditate and dwell in the truth that you find in the pages. Make the commitment to follow and use the study <u>daily</u> on your journey to true transformation.

Throughout the study, you will find different sections beginning with a heading that will guide you to understanding your transformation. Please take extra time to grasp the concept and allow your heart to truly be transformed and renewed. In the back of this booklet, there are supplemental meal plans, an exercise calendar and workouts. I encourage you to start using these today to enhance your total transformation.

Understand:

To perceive the meaning of; grasp the idea of; comprehend. In these sections I ask you to take time to really focus on content. These sections break down key truths of God's Word, and look at the different things He says about our body, mind and spirit. Allow these sections to take root in your life, <u>understanding</u> that what our Heavenly Father says in the Bible is the foundation for a <u>total transformation</u>.

Transform:

To <u>change</u> in condition, nature, or character; convert. The Transform sections will be a little more "practical" as far as <u>instant</u> application. The Transform sections will challenge you to think, write, and make real changes to your life. To get the most out of this study, you will need to take these sections very seriously and make a conscious effort <u>to act</u> and make real, <u>positive changes</u> in your life.

Turn to the Daily Checklist and Getting Started Guide today, and begin planning your transformation journey. The meal plans, exercise calendar, and workouts are guides for you to use <u>daily</u> on your quest to *Live Transformed.*

Week One

foundation for transformation

"Don't you know that you are God's sanctuary and that the Spirit of God lives in you?"
1 Corinthians 3:16

foundation

Holding a beautiful, blue-eyed, chunky baby boy and watching a spunky 2 year old little girl chasing around our silver weimaraner puppy, I felt tears streaming down my face. I was feeling so blue and dark inside but trying to hold it all together on the outside. Never wanting to disappoint anyone.

"You're a strong woman" *I would try and reassure myself. Those words quickly faded away as I found myself in that dark place again, feeling suffocated by feelings of doubt, fear and worry.* "What is the matter? Why would you feel like this?" *I would ask myself.* "You have the picture perfect life. You have a husband who loves you, two healthy babies and a recently newfound freedom from a job that was beyond physically and mentally draining. What more could you want?"

I had recently retired from working as a CPA, a job my dad told me to get because that way I would "always have a job!". Well, it turns out he was right about that. However, I always knew that working as a CPA was far from my passion in life. I had gotten that degree and job again out of a desire to do what was expected of me and in an effort to please everyone else. I spent hours, days and weeks miserable wondering how on Earth I could be so unhappy inside of a life that was seemingly so perfect. I spent hours asking but didn't hear any answers.

Suddenly on a day like any other I heard an audible voice speak directly to me saying "Do what you love to do and glorify me in what you love".

First, I had to dig deep to realize what exactly it was that voice was talking about. What did I love? The more I thought about it, the more I kept coming back to thoughts about my body and how it was time for me to stop living in defeat and negativity and begin transforming my body, mind and spirit.

It wasn't by any means an overnight transformation, but one hour that turned into one week, then one month and before long I realized what my passions were. I realized that I longed to help women find this passion inside of them and wanted to help free them from their negative thoughts. I found freedom and true joy when I began listening to what the Lord had called me to do and stopped trying to please this world- and it all began with a small step faith and starting a journey towards a total transformation.

Memorize

"Don't you know that you are God's sanctuary and that the Spirit of God lives in you?"
1 Corinthians 3:16

Reflect

What is the main reason you want to completely transform your life? What will be your biggest obstacles in transforming your body, mind and spirit?

_____

_____

_____

_____

_____

_____

_____

_____

_____

_____

_____

_____

Day One

"I will sing to the Lord all my life; I will sing praise to my God as long as I live."
Psalm 104:33 (NIV)

Understand - Your life is a gift

Precious friend, let us start Day 1 working on accepting the body you have as a gift from above, a true gift which value has already been given. Learning to <u>balance</u> the various parts of ourselves - body, mind, and spirit - is life's journey and we need to achieve this <u>balance</u> to completely transform and grow. When all of the aspects of your body are working together in harmony, Christ is able to grow and fully mature in you. In Ephesians 4:1, Paul asks us to "<u>live</u> a life worthy of the calling we have received," and we are able to do that by dedicating our lives and bodies completely and wholeheartedly to the Lord's work. How can you begin to transform today?

Realize today your body is an amazing gift. Do you treat your body as a gift?

_____

_____

What is the best gift that has ever been given to you? Journal below how you can treat your body as a wonderful gift starting today.

_____

_____

_____

_____

_____

"...prepare your minds for service and have self-control. All your hope should be for the gift of grace that will be yours when Jesus Christ is shown to you."
1 Peter 1:13 (NCV)

Ladies, you are ready to take action! Living transformed means being intentional each day! You have received a call from God to live your life to the fullest-to be able to love and serve those around you. Our first step toward transforming your body, mind and spirit is by <u>being thankful</u> for the <u>life</u> that you already have and working each day toward cultivating healthy habits into a lifestyle that is honoring to Him.

Transform - Have a Thankful heart

Write 3 specific areas of your life you are thankful for:

1._____

2._____

3._____

Be intentional and ready for action today! Set an alarm on your phone for the next 5 days to go off at 8 am with one positive statement of what you are thankful for as a daily reminder and write that reminder here.

_____
_____
_____
_____

Your life is the most precious gift! How can you use your life *just as it is today* to love well and serve wholeheartedly?

_____
_____
_____
_____
_____
_____
_____

Focus your thoughts today on being thankful for the life you have and on being content in all you have and all that you are in Christ.

"Rejoice in the Lord always. Again, I will say: "Rejoice!"
Philippians 4:4 (ESV)

Prayer

Thank you, Lord, for my life. I am grateful you have brought me into this world. Help me to honor you in all that I do and say today. I am so thankful you have blessed me with a body, mind and spirit that seeks to honor You. Guide me along your path today. Write in your own prayer below.

_____
_____
_____
_____
_____
_____
_____

Amen

I will _____ to honor my body today.

Day Two

"Love the Lord your God with all your heart and with all your soul and with all your strength and with all your mind'; and, 'Love your neighbor as yourself."
Luke 10:27

Understand - Your life has a purpose

Your life's true purpose is to <u>love</u> and to <u>serve</u> God and use all that He has given you to help others. If we believe this statement and live this in every aspect of our lives we can find the <u>true joy</u> that Jesus promises us. We can be completely fulfilled when we use our <u>passions and abilities</u> to glorify God with our whole life. Friend, we need to know and understand what our own strengths are in this life to be able to fully live with purpose.

What do you feel are some of your strengths? What are some of your passions?

_____

_____

_____

_____

Sometimes it can be hard to talk about what we are good at, but ask yourself -- what do people thank you for? Your strengths can often show up in this area. Write below what others thank you for often.

_____

_____

_____

_____

"Each of you should use whatever gift you have received to serve others, as faithful stewards of God's grace in its various forms."
1 Peter 4:10

Think about your passions, strengths and abilities -- How can you use them to serve the Lord and others today?

_____

_____

_____

_____

_____

_____

Prayer

Lord, you have given me many gifts. Please reveal these gifts to me so I can serve and love you and others well. Open my eyes and my heart to be ready and willing for wherever you may call me to go and whatever you may call me to do. I yearn to love you with my whole heart. Teach me to love and honor you more each day.

_____

_____

_____

_____

_____

_____

_____

_____

Amen

I will _____ to serve someone today.

Day Three

"Every good and perfect gift is from above, coming down from the Father of heavenly lights, who does not change like the shifting shadows."
James 1:17

Dear friend, we are going to be learning more about our strengths and passions. First, we need to know our strengths to be able to use them to live fully. Using our own <u>personal strengths</u> when we think clearly and exercise self-control, we can look forward to the special blessings that will come to us. To make lasting life changes and truly transform into the women that God wants us to become, we need <u>clear goals</u> specifically laid out for our lives. <u>Each person has a different life purpose and passion.</u> Possibly a few of your <u>life goals</u> would be to love, to be loved, to encourage, or to serve. Let's set goals today to begin your transformation.

Transform - Set goals

Your goals form a mental road map to your success. Let's dream about what could be and then figure out how to make our dreams a reality. Why do you want to transform your life?

What are some of your specific life goals? List at least 3 below and explain.

1. _____

2. _____

3. _____

Now turn to the Transformational Health Goal Sheet (p.125) in the back of the study. Start with whole body health goals that you want to achieve in one year, then work your way back to the health goals you want to reach during the next 6 weeks. Be specific in stating exactly what broad goals you want to reach during your whole body transformation.

Sample Daily Goals

Drink 1 glass of water before eating
Do 30 minutes of exercise
Stretch 5-10 minutes
Avoid eating processed foods
Give someone a compliment
Decrease soda intake
Laugh out loud
Have quiet time
Keep a food and fitness journal

Write below 3 goals to start today

1.

2.

3.

Prayer

Heavenly Father, please guide me in setting goals I can achieve with your help. I want to know you more each day and I know that by making You a priority, I will. Transform my life one day at a time to be able to love, serve and live my life to the fullest to glorify you.

_____
_____
_____
_____
_____
_____
_____

Amen

Day Four

"Above all else, guard your heart, for everything you do flows from it."
Proverbs 4:23

Now I understand, friend, that as women guarding our hearts is easier said than done. To truly guard our heart and be protected from all of the "worldliness" around us we need help from our closest circle of friends. Having accountability from a person or a few people who will support you to walk in this journey is the key to staying on track throughout your transformation.

Transform - Accountability

Spend time today praying about a person who could be your accountability partner throughout this journey. Your partner will help you in reaching your health and life goals by walking alongside you through both amazing and difficult times. Your accountability partner could be someone who has a similar mindset and goals and achieving total body health and wellness.

Write one or a few names here.

_____
_____
_____
_____

Honest, transparent accountability with God, yourself and a partner will unlock the key to complete transformation. Now take the time to text or call them and ask if they would join you in this journey! Journal about your conversation here.

_____

_____

_____

_____

_____

_____

How can you connect with this person weekly to be able to stay committed to reaching your goals together? Plan to connect with your accountability partner like a weekly appointment you can not miss!

_____

_____

_____

_____

_____

Spend some time in prayer for your accountability partner or ask God to reveal the right person to help you along this journey. Write your prayer below.

_____

_____

_____

_____

_____

_____

_____

_____

Amen

Day Five

"I pray that you may prosper in every way and be in good health, just as your soul prospers."
3 John 1:2

Sweet sister, since we now have a foundation for transformation and are beginning to recognize our strengths, passions and goals! Awesome start! **How do we honor God in our bodies in order to live our best life?**

In the first epistle of Paul to the Corinthians, he calls the people to a new life, a life not shaped by culture but by truth. Paul affirms that God lives in each of us. We worship Him by living in His presence with every aspect of our lives, whether it's physical, mental, spiritual or emotional. Spiritually, it is often easy to recognize areas we need to change or could improve on, however, changing our perspective to see our bodies as an instrument of worship can be more challenging. We need to ask God daily to change our minds.

Transform - Honor Your Body

A way we can honor God with our bodies is by cultivating healthy habits that treat our bodies with care. How can you make healthy habits? You can cultivate healthy habits by doing something *daily* that you want to change. Changing your lifestyle is not only about getting a leaner, healthier body; it is about glorifying God. Treat your body with the love and respect that a temple of the Holy Spirit deserves. Your body is an instrument of worship!

List 5 healthy habits you want to accomplish daily that will help you honor your body and transform your life:

1.

2.

3.

4.

5.

Write these 5 habits on a note card and post it in various places where you will see it every day.

Prayer

Lord, I seek to honor you with my body, mind and spirit. I want to take care of the temple you have given me but some days seem so hard. I am asking you now Lord to take this journey with me one day at a time. Small steps forward can lead to a transformed life by walking with you by my side. Thank you for this opportunity to learn more about you and live for your glory.

_____
_____
_____
_____
_____
_____
_____
_____

Amen

Day Six

Why do you desire to be Transformed?

Spend some time praying that God will use these truths to transform you. What thoughts, prayers, expectations and desires have you discovered in the last 5 days?

_____
_____
_____
_____
_____
_____

Prayer

Lord, open my eyes to see your greater purpose for my life. I long to be transformed by you. Give me courage to let go of false, negative thoughts about my body and life. Forgive me for allowing those thoughts to cross my mind. Give me the complete courage and peace to move forward that only you can give.

_____
_____
_____
_____
_____

Amen

Day Seven

Use today to reflect on the past week and prepare for the week ahead. What did you learn and do well this week? What are your new goals for this upcoming week?

_____
_____
_____
_____
_____
_____

Take the time to use the exercise calendar and meal plan guide located in the back of this book. Use them to get organized and plan for the week ahead so you can make it the best week possible! Remember sweet friend to take this journey one hour, day and week at a time.

Prayer

Heavenly Father, all power is given to you in heaven. Transform my understandings and my heart. Help me appreciate this if you have given me and help me treat it as the best gift. Cleanse my body and send your spirit into my soul so I can live as one with You today.

_____
_____
_____
_____
_____

Amen

Week Two

Your Body is a Temple

"You were bought at a price. Therefore honor God with your bodies."
1 Corinthians 6:19-20

Body

"Caroline Harris"

I remember it like it was yesterday. I can hear those words from the judge as she raised her hand signaling that it was my turn to step out onto the gymnastics floor in my tight white leotard. Of course it had to be white. Doesn't white just seem to show every single imperfection, especially in a skin tight leotard? I will never forget how incredibly self conscious I felt every time I put on a leotard and, now that I think about it, any clothing at all.

Why do we as women talk and think so badly about ourselves? We look in the mirror ready to criticize our legs, stomachs, arms, chest- any aspect of our bodies, really.

"This is too small, too big, too droopy..." You know the thoughts. Negative comments can consume our entire mind and can turn any sunny day into a dark one in the blink of an eye. We step on the scale and all of the sudden it's like our entire state of mind can change in an instant depending on if we like or don't like a singly number. Believe me sister I have been there. It's a daily struggle to not be there. Each and every day I have to battle just like you to quiet the voices in my head and truly be thankful and appreciate the body that I have been given. It's a daily task when I wake up in the morning to ask God to transform my thoughts about my body and change my perspective.

Memorize

"Do you not know that your bodies are a temple of the Holy Spirit, who is in you? You are not your own, you were bought at a price. Therefore, honor God with your bodies."

1 Corinthians 6:19-20

Reflect

Body image is the mental picture we create in our own minds of what we think we look like. Typically, our own body image does not fall in line with how others actually see us. One statistic that astounds me is only 4% of women consider themselves "beautiful." "Fat" talk among women is the norm and as women age, "old" talk joins in with it. It seems that since we were young girls, we have tended to focus on the negative aspects of our body, and our body image has become more false and untrue as we age.

We have led ourselves to believe over time that our body just isn't good enough. The only way to overcome these issues we all face with body image is to have our beliefs about our body image become transformed by the Holy Spirit. Remember, you and I are created in the image of God. We are called to reflect His image to the world! Since the fall of Adam and Eve, we have let the world's image of "beauty" take over and warp our minds.

The only way to overcome these issues we all face with body image is to have our beliefs about our body image become transformed by the Holy Spirit. <u>Remember, you and I are created in the image of God</u>. We are called to reflect His image to the world! Since the fall of Adam and Eve, we have let the world's image of "beauty" take over and warp our minds.

Paul writes in his letter to the Corinthians: "we were bought at a price." Those words are so powerful as Paul reminds us Jesus became our sin so that we could become clean and pure. God makes us beautiful with the true beauty of his Son, Jesus.

By viewing yourself though God's image, you can truly be transformed. How can you trust and believe in this statement? Take off the blurry glasses of the world and start today by allowing the Holy Spirit to transform your vision of real beauty!

_____

_____

_____

_____

_____

_____

_____

Rewrite the theme verse for week two here

_____

_____

_____

_____

_____

_____

Day One

*"Don't you know that <u>you</u> yourselves are God's temple
and that God's Spirit lives in you?"*
1 Corinthians 3:16

Lovely friend, taking proper care of your body is a form of worship to the Lord. Treating your body well can not only extend your lifespan, but improve your quality of day to day living and allow you to serve God faithfully. We need to be good stewards of the earthly bodies that we have been given by keeping it healthy and by equipping it to serve the Lord.

I get so excited thinking that one day we will have an amazing, perfect body in heaven! Have hope and peace today, trusting His plan and trusting in the vision of heaven that He gives. However, the picture of a perfect, healthy body in heaven should not open the door for us to neglect our earthly bodies. *Your body is the vessel that God uses everyday to carry out His good works.*

Understand - Your Body is a Temple

> *"You were bought with a price, therefore honor God with your body."*
> *1 Corinthians 6:20*

Yes, we all know we should treat our bodies well but <u>why</u> should you treat your body with care? What is your motivation to honor your body?

_____

_____

_____

How do you *currently* respect your body? Write specifically what you do on a <u>daily</u> basis to respect your body.

_____
_____
_____

How can you respect your body more starting today? Don't waste another hour! List 3 things you can do today to honor God with your body.

1.

2.

3.

This week, set an alarm on your phone for 10 am and 3 pm with the verse 1 Corinthians 3:16 as a reminder to honor your body.

Prayer

Lord, help me to honor you with every aspect of my body. Guide each and every choice I make and help me to give <u>You</u> complete control over how I treat my body. When I am stempted, show me how I can honor You instead. Thank you for loving me, protecting me, and guiding me.

_____
_____
_____

Amen

Today I will: Drink more water, exercise and eat more real foods.

Day Two

"By the power that enables him to bring everything under his control, he will transform our lowly bodies so that they will be like his glorious body."
Philippians 3:21

Sweet sister, when you hear the word <u>body</u>, especially in today's culture, you tend to immediately begin focusing on one thing: *body image*. And yes, body image is certainly a large part of our bodies. However, it is not by any means the full picture. Today's world seems to place more significance on how we look on the outside than who we are on the inside! The truth is, magazines, television, and the Internet, show disproportionate, airbrushed women. God's word teaches us truth! Replace these lies with truth.

"Do not conform to the patterns of this world, be transformed by the renewing of your mind." Romans 12:2

I realize this will be difficult as most of us grimace when we think of certain parts of our bodies, but please list 3 of your <u>favorite</u> body parts and spend time giving God thanks for the body and the unique parts that only you have!

1._____

2._____

3._____

Now, journal <u>honestly</u> about an issue you face in regards to your body. Most women have something that bothers them or that they wish were different, so take some time to honestly address how you feel about your body. There is such power is writing down your thoughts and/or speaking them out loud.

_____
_____
_____

Our body is so much more than just how it looks on the outside. What we can <u>do with our body</u> and how we can <u>use our body</u> for God's glory is most important! Scripture reminds us that the body is one unit, though it is made up of many parts, and all of its many parts form <u>one body</u>, so it is with Christ.

> *"Just as a body, though one, has many parts, but all its many parts form one body, so it is with Christ. For we were all baptized by one Spirit so as to form one body—whether Jews or Gentiles, slave or free—and we were all given the one Spirit to drink. Even so the body is not made up of one part but of many."*
> *1 Corinthians 12:12-14*

Transform - Shift Your Thoughts

What can you do daily to transform your negative thoughts about your body? Write below three positive statements you can recite to yourself daily.

1._____

2._____

3._____

God's transforming love is beyond our understanding. How He divinely made each one of us perfect and unique is astounding! Let the words from 1 Corinthians 12:12-14 sink into your spirit and spend time thinking about the miracle you are!

Prayer

God, thank you for creating me beautiful in your eyes. With your help, I can have a healthy body, equipped to be used for your glory. Every day help me to celebrate my unique body and focus on my strengths rather than my flaws. Thank you for making me exactly the way you planned for a special purpose. Today, cleanse my spirit and give me a pure heart, infusing positive words of affirmation into my mind about my body.

_____

_____

_____

Amen

Day Three

"For we are God's workmanship, created in Christ Jesus to do good works, which God prepared <u>in advance</u> for us to do."
Ephesians 2:10

Everyone has imperfections. Me, you, your best friend, ultimately everyone we meet or know because the fact is: we live in a broken world. However, to stay focused on our goals we must remember our created purpose is to let God's light shine through <u>every aspect</u> of our lives, expressing His beauty through our lives. ***You were created perfectly and made to shine!***

When you appreciate your unique features, abilities, and strengths, you can live out the purpose you were created for - and truly transform into a sparkling, bright light of real, everlasting beauty!

Remember - Your goal in life is not a number on a scale.

No matter what is holding you back, God's plan is prepared for you in advance to fulfill His glory. Remember that you are taking this journey <u>one day at a time</u>. Step by step you will be able to achieve your goals with <u>commitment</u> and <u>discipline</u>.

Transform - Make Healthy Habits

Last week you clearly define your personal goals for health and fitness. ***<u>You should review these goals each day</u>.*** To reach your goals you need to create and <u>maintain</u> healthy habits that you can practice daily. Write your goals on a note card and post it around your space as a constant reminder!

What healthy habits have you formed in the past 10 days?

_____

_____

_____

_____

_____

Victory! Great job, lovely lady! Small steps can lead to big results! Keep motivated!

What can you do <u>more of</u> or <u>differently</u> this week to honor your body and achieve your goals?

1._____

2._____

3._____

4._____

Research shows it takes at least 30 days to change a habit and to develop a new one.

As we have discussed already, making good choices daily will have a significant impact on reaching your goals. This verse in James shows how connected <u>prayer</u> and <u>dependence on God</u> are for a healthy body. We need to depend on God to help us make good choices.

"If any of you lacks wisdom, <u>you should ask God</u>, who gives generously to all without finding fault, and it will be given to you. But when you ask, you must believe and not doubt, because the one who doubts is like a wave of the sea, blown and tossed by the wind." James 1:5-6

The healthy habits I will practice today to promote my healthy body image are:

1.

2.

3.

Prayer

Lord, thank you that your Word says I am fearfully and wonderfully made. I need your strength when I am tempted so that I can make the best choices today. I ask for your encouragement as I strive to reach my goals. Continue to transform my body, mind and spirit each day so I can honor you in all I do. I will trust in your perfect plan for my whole body. Please allow your love and light to shine brightly through me today.

_____
_____
_____

Amen

Day Four

"As iron sharpens iron, so a friend sharpens a friend."
Proverbs 27:17

Beautiful friend, support and encouragement of family and friends are vital in your total transformation. As shown in the book of Proverbs, there is a mutual benefit when two iron blades rub together. The edges become sharper and more efficient. Also, the sharp knife will shine more if the dull residue has been rubbed away. The proverb teaches us that we (especially as women) need and crave fellowship and are strengthened by one another. Sometimes it is not easy and may seem uncomfortable to be an encourager, but today your challenge is to go outside of your comfort zone and encourage someone with affirming, positive words!

Transform - Maintain Accountability

Have you checked in with your accountability partner this week? If not, try to connect today and talk openly about any struggles you have been having. Can you talk honestly with your partner about your own body image? Write about your conversation and how you can work together with your accountability partner or a friend to reach your goals.

_____
_____
_____
_____

What can you do <u>today</u> to "sharpen" a friend?

_____
_____
_____

Spend time throughout the day praying about how you can encourage a friend and help her learn about maintaining a healthy lifestyle and body image.

Prayer

Father, I praise you because you have made me beautiful and perfect in your sight. You have woven me together so perfectly and you have removed a veil of darkness from my face so that I might reflect a bright light to others. I want to encourage a friend today. Show me how to use my entire body to live boldly for you.

_____

_____

_____

Amen

Day five

"There are six days when you may work, but the seventh day is a day of Sabbath rest, a day of sacred assembly. You are not to do any work; wherever you live, it is a Sabbath to the Lord."
Leviticus 23:3

Don't we all take proper rest for granted? I know I do! Does your mind sometimes seem foggy? It is often in those times that we start a downward spiral in our healthy habits in every area: body, mind and spirit. Rest is so important to strengthen our whole body. When starting a new wellness plan to increase your fitness, your body needs at least one day for rest and recovery. Your body is beautiful and was created uniquely for a special purpose. Allowing time for rest will give you the energy needed to carry out that purpose.

Understand - Rest in the Lord

Finding our strength in God and honoring Him by having a rest day is vital for your transformation. Through proper rest you will have the mental clarity to focus on your goals and strive for progress. Trust that He will transform your body, mind and spirit while you rest. Rest in God's strength and believe that His plan will work for your good.

Take physical inventory: How was your rest this week? How many hours on average do you sleep nightly?

_____

_____

_____

```
┌─────────────────────────────────────────┐
│           Sleep/Rest tips                 │
│         Try an Epsom Salt Bath            │
│       Use Lavender Essential Oils         │
│           Drink  Magnesium                │
│     Enjoy a glass of warm Chamomile Tea   │
│    Take time to enjoy deep, calming breaths│
│   Try no TV, no phone, or computer screens 30│
│         minutes before  bedtime           │
└─────────────────────────────────────────┘
```

Rest is a key element to our mental and physical health. For ideal health, 7-9 hours is recommended. In Genesis we see that even God Himself took a day of rest after He finished His creation. We are human and have to humble ourselves before the Lord and not push our bodies to a point where we are neglecting our rest. Take some extra time this week to really focus on getting the proper rest that your body requires. Trust me, your body will thank you!

Transform - Give Yourself Rest

How can you focus more on rest today and this week? List specifically 3 things you can do to focus on better rest this week.

1.

2.

3.

Prayer

Lord, I need your strength today when I am weak. I have many challenges with trying to eat clean, exercise, and rest and many days it seems impossible. Help me to experience true joy in you today. I want to rest in your peace and love and trust in your plan for my health. Give me the ability to be patient and thankful in all circumstances. Draw me closer to you and give me strength to make the right choices.

_____

_____

_____

Amen

Add a "rest" goal to your goal worksheet

Today I will rest more by:_____

_____

Day Six

Are you Living Transformed?

Spend some time praying about what you have learned through this study thus far with regard to your total transformation. Is God changing the way you view your body image? How?

Prayer

Lord, open my eyes to see your greater purpose for my life. I long to be transformed by you. Give me courage to let go of false, negative thoughts about my body image. Infuse my spirit with your love and peace. Give me boldness and courage to move forward so that I can glorify you.

Amen

Day Seven

Use today to look at the exercise calendar and meal plan for the week ahead. Prepare for a successful, healthy week by getting organized. Make an exercise plan you can commit to this week. Prepare your meal plan to set yourself up for victory this week.

_____

_____

_____

_____

_____

Prayer

Lord, all power is given to you in heaven. You alone can transform my body, mind and spirit to become more like you. Help me appreciate my life and my unique body. Create in me a clean heart so that I can honor you fully with my body.

Continue to pray today about accepting your body as it was given to you and about how you can use your body to love and serve your Heavenly Father.

_____

_____

_____

_____

_____

Amen

Week Three

Nutrition is Vital

"Whatever you eat or drink, do it all for the glory of God."
1 Corinthians 10:31

Nutrition

"Nawlins" - that's where I came from. Home of the pralines, crawfish, etouffee, jambalaya and all things delicious and completely non-nutritious. PaPah's (my stepfather) love language is to love you by feeding you with all things delicious: butter, bacon, mayo and anything else that makes your heart skip a beat (sometimes quite literally). So growing up I didn't always have the healthiest eating habits. In college I worked with a nutritionist to become a better athlete but it was never something that came naturally to me because it wasn't the way that I grew up. Today I talk continually with my three children about moderation because I want them to know that eating real foods with treats in moderation makes us feel better and having a healthy body honors God.

Memorize

"Whatever you eat or drink, do it all for the glory of God."
1 Corinthians 10:31

Reflect

Do we honestly eat and drink for God's glory or do we do it for our own fulfillment? How do we remove food as an idol from our lives and begin to treat it as an instrument of God's glory?

_____

_____

_____

_____

_____

_____

_____

_____

_____

_____

_____

_____

_____

Day One

"Their destiny is destruction, their god is their stomach, and their glory is in their shame. Their mind is set on earthly things... He will transform our bodies so that they will be like His glorious body."
Philippians 3:19-21

Transform - Develop New Habits

Friends, let's start today by working to develop a new relationship with food! Food is a part of life-- NOT the reason for life. Food is something that is meant to fuel our bodies so that we are able to do the good works laid out for us! Yes, God gave us food that is wonderfully delicious so we can enjoy His many blessings. However, when food becomes an idol or an obstacle that hinders our bodies from working instead of nourishing, this is a sign we need to <u>change our perspective and relationship with our nutrition</u>.

Starting a hand written food journal or trying an app like MyFitnessPal is a great way to hold yourself accountable. To change your nutrition for the better, you need to first understand and know what type of foods and food quantities you are consuming. When we educate ourselves as to what is going <u>into</u> our bodies, then we can begin to work to make positive changes. *Has your struggle with food ever caused you any problems physically, emotionally, or spiritually? Be honest as you explain your history with food.*

_____

_____

_____

_____

How can you change this battle with food for good?

_____

_____

_____

_____

_____

If you haven't started a food journal, start one today and commit to journaling honestly what you are eating and drinking daily. Pray about sharing the journal with your accountability partner.

Try to add color to each meal shooting for 7-10 servings of fruit and vegetables per day.

> *"But food does not bring us near to God; we are no worse if we do not eat, and no better if we do."*
> *1 Corinthians 8:8*

Prayer

Lord, thank you for providing us with a bounty of wonderful, nutritious foods. Help me to crave time with you, not certain foods. Fill my body and spirit with your love and peace when I am tempted to overindulge. I want to release my struggle with food today and be filled with your presence.

_____

_____

_____

Amen

I will: <u>set a goal this week to journal honestly about nutrition for 7 days.</u>

Day Two

"I am the vine; she is the branches. If she remains in me and I in her, she will <u>bear much fruit</u>; apart from me she can do nothing." John 15:5

Sweet sister, let this verse speak to your heart. *"Remain in me"* the Scriptures remind us; it calls us to make God the top priority. Our main goal is to walk hand in hand with God each day through every aspect of our lives. Staying organized by meal planning can assist you so that you can spend more time walking in step and staying focused. Enjoying real food in a healthy balance will help you achieve your goals while feeling your absolute best. If we desire to see results in how we look and feel, sticking to a <u>balanced</u> health and nutrition plan is essential. As we discussed in week one, there are <u>sample meal plans</u> included for you in the back of this study. They are guides to teach you how to eat a balanced, nutrient dense diet daily.

How will following one of the provided meal plans or creating your own meal plan (on the blank template) be beneficial for you? Are you able to stick with a meal plan to the best of your ability? Why or why not?

_____

_____

_____

_____

A quote from one of my favorite songs is, ***"Begin to be <u>now</u>, what you <u>will be</u> forever."*** Stop putting off what is so important to your body and <u>focus</u> on what you put <u>into</u> <u>your</u> body. There are no shortcuts to a healthy lifestyle. Today, strive to put <u>God first</u> and then take time to enjoy the foods that He has provided in <u>moderation</u>.

What is one way you take shortcuts in your life with regards to your nutrition?

_____

_____

_____

How can you stop taking shortcuts and make changes with your nutrition that will lead to lasting transformation and help you feel your best?

_____

_____

_____

Transform - Check Your Progress

Go through the Getting Started Guide list in the back of this book and work on checking off a few items you haven't yet completed. Do your best to make small changes each day to help you reach your goals. Eating a balanced breakfast is the first step in your healthy day, and healthy lifestyle.

Prayer

Lord, reside in my body and help me today to improve my nutrition. With your help, I know I can succeed in meal planning and eating foods that nourish my body, mind and spirit. Help me to see that this is not simply a diet, but a lifestyle change, so I can treat my temple with respect and care. I want to turn to you today in prayer when I am tempted. Fill my body with your love and nourishment. Remain in me Holy Spirit and walk by my side today. Amen

Day Three

"For we have been saved through <u>faith</u>, and this is not from yourselves, it is the gift of God."
Ephesians 2:8

You are beautiful! Yes, sister, now is the time to break free from the past! We have been saved through faith! Each day we need to take small steps and move in the right direction by making new <u>healthy</u> habits with our nutrition- not through quick fixes like diet pills, fad diets, or the latest "fitness" craze. As it says in Romans 3:23, we <u>all</u> fall short and make mistakes along this journey but don't let one slip-up ruin your new healthy lifestyle. Move forward; <u>clean the slate</u> and recommit to your healthy lifestyle today!

> ***"...for all have sinned and fall short of the glory of God"***
> ***Romans 3:23***

Write 3 parts of your life that would be changed for the better if you ate more nutritious foods:

1._____
2._____
3._____

Yesterday is gone; tomorrow is yet to come-- focus on today! The journey to <u>living transformed</u> may not be easy, but it is <u>more than worth it</u>! Ask for God's help every step of the way.

> ***"So I say to you: ask and it will be given to you; seek and you will find; knock and the door will be opened to you."***
> ***Luke 11:9***

Understand - Ask and it will be Given

Write below what nutrition habits help you feel your best. Drinking enough water daily is one that you can start today. Will you first, ask God and second, ask your accountability partner to help you maintain these habits?

_____
_____
_____
_____

Transform - Start Fresh

You will find in the back of this book that there are 10 tips to cleaning the slate and starting fresh. Read and check off the items you can or already do to help your transformation journey. Continue to use your meal plan as a guide and journal about your nutrition daily.

-Water-

Fresh, abundant and free! Your body is made up of 50-70% water, making it a key nutrient that is vital to our bodies. Let's focus on getting a minimum of 64 oz daily.

Prayer

Lord, forgive me for any bad choices I might have made that dishonor the beautiful body you have given me. Thank you for saving me and cleansing me by your grace alone. Mold me into the person you want me to be! I long to serve you fully, and I can by honoring my body with the bounty of foods you provide. I ask that you give me strength as I seek to accomplish this task. Work and move in my life to help make lasting changes.

_____

_____

_____

_____

_____

_____

Amen

Day Four

"You satisfy me more than the richest feast. I will praise you with songs of joy."
Psalms 63:5

Amazing sister, you are working so hard to live a transformed life. ***Stay focused***! I believe you can achieve your goals! God has blessed you with His creation that is full of wonderful things. Celebrating all the delicious foods you *can* eat rather than the foods that we shouldn't eat should be your focus today.

Try to eat foods that are created by God to nourish your body- less processed, boxed items. A super foods list is provided in your study. Do you have some of these items in your pantry? If so, list a few you can use this week. Also, write how you can use more super foods regularly in your nutrition plan.

_____

_____

_____

_____

Be proud of the great things you already do! What foods do you eat regularly that are good for your body? Add these foods into your next weekly meal plan along with a few new super foods to try.

_____

_____

_____

_____

_____

What foods do you need to eliminate or limit from your nutrition plan to be able to reach your goals? Do you need to work on portion control? Talk with your accountability partner about how you can make this change.

_____

_____

_____

_____

Why is it so important that you make your nutrition a priority?

_____

_____

_____

_____

Scripture asks us to offer our whole selves without reservation to God. Back in Week 1, we referenced how it takes at least 30 days to make a lasting change, so do not be discouraged if any one of your goals takes longer than you would like.

> **_Remember to strive for progress each day, not perfection._**

Transform - Start Today

What are 3 healthy habits with nutrition you can start today? Show this list to your accountability partner. Ask this person to help you maintain these habits.

1. _____
2. _____
3. _____

Prayer

Lord, my body is a temple. I want to glorify you through everything I eat, drink, do and say. Hep me to be thankful for the wonderful things I have and release the things holding me back from being my best self. Increase my faith and allow me to trust you completely to transform my life.

_____
_____
_____
_____
_____
_____

Amen

Day Five

"Everything that lives and moves will be food for you.
Just as I give you the plants, I now give you everything."
Genesis 9:3

Beautiful friend, you are what you eat. This is a scary but very real truth. Eating nutritious foods to build a healthy body wasn't intended to be complicated. Having good nutrition habits does take time, discipline, and accountability but it *is possible* with God's help! Decreasing empty calories such as processed foods, white breads, pastas, and sweets while increasing more nutrient dense foods such as plant foods and quality proteins will help you fuel your body so that you can live your best life and fulfill your purpose. You __can__ change with God's help and step by step you can transform your nutrition habits.

Transform - Make New Changes

How can you take "empty calories" out of your <u>daily</u> diet? What will you use to replace these foods?

_____
_____
_____
_____
_____
_____
_____

Let's write in some nutrient dense foods that <u>you enjoy</u> to build your healthy nutrition plan. Reference the super foods list in the Getting Started Guide and High Protein Snacks pages in the back of the study for assistance.

<u>Plant Foods:</u>

<u>Quality Protein:</u>

<u>Healthy Fats:</u>

<u>Vitamins/Minerals:</u>

God has given us all we need to live our best life. Are you honoring Him with what you put into your body? Check in with your accountability partner this week and talk openly about how you can reach your nutrition goals. Set a new daily goal that you want to achieve that you will do for 3 consecutive days and write it below.

_____

_____

_____

_____

_____

Set your phone alarm to remind you of this daily goal to go off around 9 am each day.

Prayer

Lord, I want to focus on you today when I feel tempted to make unhealthy choices. You can give me all I need to thrive. Strengthen my spirit and make me strong for the journey of life. I want to lean on you today when I feel weak. Help me to make the best choices with my nutrition so that I may honor you with my whole body. I will give you my best, Lord, as you have given me everything.

_____

_____

_____

_____

_____

_____

Amen

Day Six

Are you Transforming your Nutrition Habits?

Spend some time praying about what you have learned through this study so far regarding your current nutrition habits. Ask God to help you overcome whatever obstacles you face on a daily basis. Now, *write your own prayer below* and include your new healthy nutrition plan of action.

_____

_____

_____

_____

_____

_____

_____

_____

_____

How has God transformed the way you view proper nutrition and its importance in your daily life?

_____

_____

_____

_____

_____

_____

_____

_____

Day Seven

Use today to look at your exercise calendar and week ahead. Plan your exercise and write out your meal plan for the week . Commit to sticking with your plan.

Show your plans to your accountability partner. Prepare for a successful, healthy week by taking time to rest and get organized.

Write 1 Corinthians 10:31 from memory.

_____

_____

_____

_____

_____

Week four

Exercise is Worship

"...offer your bodies as a living sacrifice, holy and pleasing to God - this is your true and proper worship"
Romans 12:1

Exercise

You know, I actually hated running until a few years ago. We used to have to run "Baxter Hill" (the biggest hill in Athens) for punishment which made me began to see running as a form of punishment, and the worst form at that. So while I enjoyed exercise I by no means enjoyed all types of exercise. Beach walks and runs are now my favorite form because I feel that my mind truly opens and is clear when I can run with the wind in my face. I go until I don't think I can take another step and then God gives me that strength to keep going. I can feel His hand against my back pushing me and supporting me with every step. It's when I truly started to see God's presence in exercise that it stopped being a punishment and began to be a tool He could use to give me life, energy and strength.

Memorize

"...offer your bodies as a living sacrifice, holy and pleasing to God- this is your true and proper worship."
Romans 12:1

Reflect

While eating nutritious foods is vitally important for your health, adding activity into your daily routine is important as well. God gave us bones, muscles and joints and designed our bodies perfectly to move! If some of your goals are to lose body fat and to gain energy so you can be more ready to love and serve, then aerobic activity is another key to unlocking your success. Regular exercise will create a positive energy cycle and allow you to feel your best.

Encourage your family and friends to be active with you. Remember all forms of movement add up and will help you maintain a healthy body image, composition, and energy level. Even on your busiest days try to do something physical! What are some things you can do throughout the day to move more? 10 minutes is always better than no minutes!

_____

_____

Aerobic exercises, strength and body weight exercises, and flexibility exercises are the three major areas of physical fitness. Your goal is to incorporate these exercises into your daily routine. Developing a healthy attitude toward exercise is the first step to victory!

What is one way you can shift your attitude towards exercise today?

_____

_____

_____

Decide today to make exercise a <u>daily</u> lifestyle habit. Make exercise enjoyable and make a daily appointment with yourself. Say to yourself, "I am making exercise a daily habit. I am learning to see my goals and my body through God's eyes." Honestly, why is it that you need to make exercise a daily habit? How will you achieve this goal in the days ahead?

_____

_____

_____

_____

_____

_____

Day One

*"Jesus said to him, Away from me, Satan! For it is written:
<u>Worship</u> the Lord your God, and serve him only."
Matthew 4:10*

Dear friend, don't we want to give our best effort in this life? Preparing our bodies to be physically fit is a way of ensuring that we can truly give our best – a way to be ready to work for His glory! Our bodies can serve us to help us live more <u>meaningful</u> and <u>productive</u> lives for the Lord.

We are called to weave worship into every aspect of life. Fitness and movement can be a powerful form of worship! By seeking to improve our physical bodies, we are honoring God by taking care of the amazing body that He blessed us with. How do we do this exactly? We can start by making <u>fitness goals</u> and a <u>practical plan</u> of action.

Transform - Develop New Habits

Refer to the workouts located in the back of this study. Make changes to the plan to make it your own. If you haven't already, try one of the workouts. Which one did you attempt? How did you feel?

_____
_____
_____

How can you make this goal of <u>routine</u> exercise a reality? (Plan workouts with a friend, make a weekly schedule, get up earlier in the mornings, etc.) Write out your exercise plan for this week here.

_____

_____

_____

Write <u>how</u> you can view exercise as a form of worship.

_____

_____

_____

_____

Prayer

Lord, I want to use my body to love and serve. Equip me with the discipline to maintain my exercise routine so that my body will be strong and bring glory to you. Thank you for allowing me the opportunity to use exercise as a form of worship.

_____

_____

_____

Amen

I will plan my exercise for the week ahead ☐
I will enjoy exercise as a form of worship ☐
I will stretch my body today ☐

Day Two

"So let us not get tired of doing good, for at just the right time we will reap a harvest of blessing if we don't give up."
Galatians 6:9

As many of us know, exercise can be difficult. Sometimes being unmotivated to workout is natural- but don't give in! Research shows that it takes the fascia in your muscles 15-20 minutes to glide smoothly. Start with a goal of 15-20 minutes of exercise when you aren't feeling your best and once you get started, your body will begin to release endorphins to help you finish feeling strong and confident, while also boosting your mood.

Finding the *right balance* regarding exercise is what scripture suggests.

Exercise is a way to strengthen your muscles while clearing your head and lifting your spirits. Do you *honestly* feel that exercise can lift your mood? How?

_____

_____

_____

Write how you feel after you have exercised for 30 minutes. Do you feel stronger? More confident?

_____

_____

_____

_____

_____

What is your struggle with exercise? Time, location, resources? Write below your exercise obstacles and ways to overcome these today. Talk with your partner about these obstacles.

_____

_____

_____

Prayer

Heavenly Father, help me to not get weary as I pursue a healthier lifestyle to honor you. I know that you are preparing me to work for your kingdom. I seek to know you more each day. Please help me to not give up when I feel tired and unmotivataed. I want to worship you with my whole body.

_____

_____

_____

Amen

I will be grateful for the body I have that allows me to exercise. ☐

> **"Let me hear joy and gladness; let the bones you have crushed rejoice."**
> **Psalm 51:8**

**How much exercise is regular exercise? American College of Sports Medicine recommends 150 minutes of exercise per

Day Three

"Every day they continued to meet together in the temple courts. They broke bread in their homes and ate together with glad and sincere hearts, praising God and enjoying the favor of all the people. And the Lord added to their number daily those who were being saved."
Acts 2:46-47

Beautiful friend, once again, following a specific exercise plan and having an accountability partner to help you reach your goals will help you stay dedicated to your health and wellness plan. You will exercise more often and stay committed if you <u>love what you do</u> and you <u>have accountability</u> to follow through with your goals. Plan to check in with your accountability partner today!

What types of exercise do you enjoy? List activities you enjoy below and place a star by your favorites.

_____

_____

_____

_____

_____

Take this time to check in with your accountability partner. Write about how having accountability has helped you in reaching your goals.

_____

_____

_____

_____

_____

Transform - Exercise Together

Can you and your accountability partner make time to do one of your favorite activities this week?

_____

_____

_____

Prayer

Father, You are the one that I need to fill my spirit-not worldly things! Help me to encourage my accountability partner. Search me, Lord, and reveal to me how I can be transformed for your glory. Walk by my side as I stay committed to honoring my body through all types of worship.

_____

_____

_____

Amen

I will exercise for 30 minutes 5 times this week ☐

Day Four

"Finally, be strong in the Lord and in his mighty power."
Ephesians 6:10

Understand - Strength comes from the Lord

Where do you find strength to keep going? Living transformed means once you make a decision to do something, you make a <u>commitment</u>. Commit to whole body health and surrender each area of your life to God and ask Him to give you the <u>strength</u> to do whatever it is that you are setting out to do. Honor Him with your <u>whole body</u>. Trust that with God's help you can accomplish anything. From there, make and adjust goals.

Write down the specific goals you want to focus on for the rest of this week.

_____

_____

_____

What are some obstacles you may face in reaching your goals? How can you proactively plan to overcome these obstacles?

_____

_____

_____

_____

_____

_____

_____

When the times get tough, don't run to the pantry for comfort - run to the Lord and pick up Scripture for encouragement! Next, re-read the goals that you wrote down and reflect below on the commitments you made and why you made them in the first place. Remind yourself that you can truly do <u>ALL</u> things through <u>Christ</u> who gives you strength, and that means ALL! Let's make the decision to keep doing what is right, and the <u>results will come</u> if we commit to not giving up! Continue, beautiful friend, to strive daily for progress, not perfection.

> *"For I know the plans I have for you, declares the Lord, plans to prosper you and not to harm you, plans to give you hope and a future."*
> *Jeremiah 29:11*

Prayer

Write below your own prayer and ask the Lord to give you strength when you are weak.

_____

_____

_____

_____

_____

_____

Amen

Day Five

"No discipline seems enjoyable at the time, but painful. Later it will yield the fruit of peace and righteousness if we do not give up."
Hebrews 12:11

Inspiring friend, another way you can work at being disciplined in all areas is to commit a part of your day to the Lord in a quiet time of reading God's Word and prayer. Starting your day with a quiet time can change the direction of your day for the better. Your transformation journey should be helping you to walk with the Lord moment by moment throughout your day. Leaning on and talking with God when you feel discouraged or weak is something you need to work on in order to remain steadfast and strong. This is a crucial step along your transformational journey to whole body health.

Write down 3 practical ways that you can stay committed and be disciplined to your healthy lifestyle.

_____

_____

_____

Have you exercised (at least 30 minutes per day) in the past 3 days? How do you feel? If you haven't, ask yourself why and write that here.

_____

_____

_____

_____

_____

_____

How can you make exercise a priority in your life? Why is making exercise a priority so crucial to your healthy life-style?

_____

_____

_____

_____

_____

> **"I can do all things through Christ who gives me strength."**
> **Philippians 4:13**

Prayer

Thank you for giving me a body so that I may glorify you, Lord. I am grateful because I know that with your help I can do ALL things! Help me to stay committed to keep running the race, striving to reach my goals, and never giving up. Please encourage me, Lord, that no matter how many times I fall, you will always help me get back up. Today, I am making the decision to stay committed to living a healthy lifestyle and I know the results will come as I commit to the decision to never give up!

_____

_____

_____

_____

_____

Amen

Day Six

Have you Transformed your view of Exercise?

Spend some time praying to God about what you have learned this week about viewing exercise as a form of worship. How has God been changing the way you view exercise and how will those changes make a lasting impact in your life?

_____
_____
_____
_____
_____
_____
_____
_____
_____
_____
_____
_____

Day Seven

Use today to look at the exercise calendar, meal plan and your week ahead. Prepare for a successful, healthy week by getting organized.

Review and adjust your goals for the next two weeks to maximize your transformation.

Write a short prayer below asking God to give you His view of your amazing body today. Confess any negative thoughts you may have to Him and allow him to renew and restore those thoughts to become positive and encouraging truths. Open your heart to let His words flow through you.

_____
_____
_____
_____
_____
_____
_____
_____
_____
_____
_____
_____

Week five
Your Mind is the Center

"...finally, brothers and sisters, whatever is true, whatever is noble, whatever is right, whatever is pure, whatever is lovely, whatever is admirable - if anything is excellent or praiseworthy - think about such things."

Philippians 4:8

Mind

Does your mind tend to wander down the road of negativity some days?

"I'm not good enough to..."
"I don't look good in..."
"She is way better than me at..."

Our minds are the driving force behind what is helping us or hindering us from reaching our goals and ultimately from having true, lasting joy. There is so much truth in the quote "Comparison is the thief of joy" and I believe much of that truth comes from the fact that when we compare ourselves, it is almost always in a negative light.

*My struggles with depression are what led me to my lowest point of feeling unloved, unwanted and unsupported. However, through the depths of tears and loneliness God loved me in each moment. I can't say I felt His hand on my shoulder all the time but looking back, He was there growing and transforming me spiritually through it all. I learned the truth in Romans 8:28 when we are told that God works together **all** things for the good of those who love Him.*

What we have to do, friends, is train our minds to shift towards seeing our circumstances through God's eyes. The only way this is possible is by reading God's Word and trusting Him to change our perspective to see His plan in every circumstance. He can saturate every thought, changing grumbling into gratitude.

Reflect

One of the most important aspects to your total transformation is your thoughts, because our thoughts directly impact our actions and our future. Yes, it's true if we have negative thoughts, it is much more difficult to have a joy-filled life.

Scripture shows us in Proverbs 23:7
"As she thinks in her heart, so does she become."

As we strive to live transformed, one of the biggest obstacles we need to overcome with our mind is fixating our thoughts on idols. We all have idols that seem to control our thoughts. Let's discuss a few idols that could be controlling your thoughts and holding you back from totally transforming.

_____

_____

_____

_____

_____

_____

_____

_____

_____

_____

_____

_____

_____

_____

Overall, it is essential to shift your thoughts heavenward, away from worldly things so that your thoughts will look more like the thoughts of Jesus. Your mind is so powerful! Thoughts can and will affect who you become! Do you need to shift your daily thoughts? If so, how?

_____

_____

_____

_____

"Finally, brothers, whatever is true, whatever is noble, whatever is right, whatever is pure, whatever is lovely, whatever is admirable—if anything is excellent or praiseworthy—think about such things."
Philippians 4:8

We are called to walk in His spirit and have a joy filled life. By walking daily in step and focusing on Philippians 4:8 our mind will begin to slowly change to be filled with thoughts of gratitude and praise which can transform our entire life!

Stop! Right now - challenge yourself and your accountability partner to not speak negative words for 24 hours. Yes, the challenge is difficult but being aware of your thoughts is the first step in transforming them! You can do it!

Day One

"Set your mind on things above, not what is on the Earth."
Colossians 3:2

Beautiful friend, while exercise and nutrition are very important for a healthy lifestyle, mental health is equally as important. Finding the right balance between physical, mental and spiritual health is essential for your total transformation to occur.

Understand - Set your Mind on things Above

When transforming our whole bodies, we need to focus on our thoughts just as much as we focus on nutrition and exercise. When you can control your thoughts, you can improve your emotional strength, which is your potential for true joy. Paul reminds us in his letter to the Philippians that we need to set our minds on the amazing things of heaven, not on the things of this world.

"Finally, brothers, whatever is true, whatever is noble, whatever is right, whatever is pure, whatever is lovely, whatever is admirable—if anything is excellent or praiseworthy—think about such things."
Philippians 4:8

Stop right now-- what are you thinking? How can you focus on what you are grateful for today? Be specific and list areas of your life that you are grateful for-- list as many as possible!

_____

_____

_____

_____

_____

In regards to your <u>health</u>, what lovely or positive thoughts can you think of today? As we all struggle with negativity, I know this may be difficult, but try your best to put down <u>at least 3</u> positive thoughts about your health below.

_____

_____

_____

_____

When your thoughts start to spiral downward, try to stop yourself and remember what you have written above. Allow yourself to feel that gratitude again, and begin to practice shifting your thoughts towards gratitude and thanksgiving. Write Philippians 4:8 down here in your own words and strive to commit this verse to memory this week. What does this verse mean to you?

_____

_____

_____

_____

Transform - Change Your Thoughts

Be intentional about changing your thoughts: set an alarm on your phone to go off 3 times throughout the day that says "Philippians 4:8!"

I will repeat throughout the day - "I am beautiful in the eyes of the Lord" ☐

I will shift my mind to thoughts of heaven ☐

Prayer

Compose your own prayer here, asking God to help you see yourself the way that He sees you and describes you in His Word. Sister, you are beautifully and wonderfully made in the image of the Almighty God!

_____
_____
_____
_____
_____

Amen

Day Two

"Commit your works to the Lord and your thoughts will be established."
Proverbs 16:3

The old saying is true, as the mind goes, so goes the body. By setting our minds on our <u>specific goals</u> and walking in the Spirit <u>daily,</u> we can stay focused. Paul reminds us in the book of Philippians that when things are going well we find it easy to offer praise to God, but when times are hard, we find it difficult to worship and give thanks to Him. Do you find this to be true in your life? I <u>definitely</u> do! However, we must stay focused on the <u>truth</u> that we can do ALL things through Christ who will give us <u>strength</u> to get through whatever circumstances may come our way. Ladies, let's change our thoughts to focus on Christ and the many blessings He gives us instead of pushing thoughts of Him aside when times are tough. As strong women, we need to shift our focus <u>heavenward</u> and allow Him to be our source of strength.

Friend, I understand that the hard part is letting go of negative thoughts about our bodies! We need to start by releasing the past and focusing on the present. What matters most each day in our quest for a transformed life is ***<u>not the body from our past but what we are doing with our bodies today!</u>***

Yes! You can worship and glorify God with _any_ body type starting today! Because of this grace, each day is a fresh start and an opportunity to worship and serve with not only your body, but your entire being: body, mind and spirit. Living a transformed life isn't only about changing your bodily appearance, nutrition habits, or even your fitness- it is about being set free by God's _unending_ and _abounding_ love. God has already set you free from the negative chains of your past and gives you freedom to worship Him by dedicating your body, a _temple_, for His glory!

Do negative thoughts cross your mind daily about your body? Write these thoughts down so that you can _let go_ of what may be holding you back from reaching your goals. Release these thoughts now!

_____

_____

_____

_____

Now let's work to shift your negative thoughts to positive ones. I understand this is not easy, but I encourage you to take time now to write at least _two positive statements_ about your body.

_____

_____

_____

_____

_____

Beautiful friend, I believe in you and know you can start fresh and shift your thoughts to positive ones today!

Transform - think Positive thoughts

Say out loud 3x today the positive statements you have written earlier. Write them on a note card to post around your house and work.

Prayer

Lord, I confess I am not pure and I am not without fault. By your grace, please cleanse my heart and cleanse my thoughts. Purify me until I am clean in your eyes. Transform my mind and spirit so that I can glorify you with my whole body. I want to focus on the present moment. Help me to be grateful for everyday blessings and glorify you.

_____

_____

_____

_____

_____

Amen

Day Three

"... give thanks in <u>all</u> circumstances; for this is God's will for you in Christ Jesus."
1 Thessalonians 5:18

Developing mental discipline is very difficult, but it truly is the key to a total life transformation. Sadly, developing mental strength doesn't happen overnight. Let go of the negative thoughts that are pulling you down and ask the Holy Spirit to give you strength where you need it most. If you want to gain emotional control, you must first gain control of your mind, which is only possible through God's help. When our minds are renewed, we can be truly transformed by God's power and love. Focusing daily on the many strengths and blessings you have will help you remain focused and develop the mindset that God longs for you to have. Do this now by writing out 3 blessings in your life. This could be a person, an object or an entire area of your life. Focus on your blessings here.

1.

2.

3.

Developing mental discipline is the key in a total life transformation.

> *"Therefore do not worry about tomorrow, for tomorrow will worry about itself. Each day has enough trouble of its own."*
> *Matthew 6:34*

Take time here to reflect and pray. Have you ever struggled with depression, anxiety, or specific fears? Write below any mental struggles you have dealt with and how you can create your own comeback story. Give your comeback story a positive ending!

_____

_____

_____

_____

_____

_____

_____

Transform - Be Vulnerable

If you feel comfortable, talk with your accountability partner today about the paragraph above. I know this will be difficult, but being transparent can help you in your journey to living transformed.

Prayer

Lord, some days I have no enthusiasm but rather a heavy heart and an overwhelming feeling that seems contagious. Reassure me today that I am not alone. I give you this day, Lord; I lay down all of my worries to you. I put this day into your hands. Thank you for taking on my burdens. I can rest peacefully knowing that you can handle anything and your love is faithful and true. Amen.

Day Four

"Be completely humble and gentle; be patient, bearing with one another in love. Make every effort to keep the unity of the Spirit through the bond of peace."
Ephesians 4:2-3

The individuals you habitually spend time with will influence who you eventually become as a person. You will either be sharpened or dulled by the people you surround yourself with each day. Sweet friend, try to build healthy relationships with people who lift you up and encourage you. Celebrate life by spending time with those who inspire you! How can you work to build healthier relationships? What can you do specifically this week to build a relationship?

_____
_____
_____
_____

List 3 relationships with people who enrich your life and write how you can nurture these
relationships:

1.

2.

3.

To fully experience God's gifts you need up-lifting, loving people to share life with daily. Let us seek to be the joy-filled women in others' lives by encouraging others in new ways!

Smile; give a high five or a true compliment! You never know when a small bit of encouragement will give someone the strength to do what they feel they cannot do and try what they might not dare to try. It may not seem like much at the time but it's planting a seed of hope and light into someone's life that could mean everything. Being honest and transparent can help build relationships. How can you share your experiences with others in a way that will encourage or inspire them?

_____

_____

_____

_____

_____

Transform - Speak Kind Words

Who will you encourage today and what will you do or say to encourage a friend?

_____

_____

Prayer

Lord, show me how I can encourage others by showing them your love. Help me become a bright light for you!
Thank you, Lord, for the relationships in my life that encourage me and that continually point me to you.

_____

_____

Amen

Day five

"Do not conform to the pattern of this world, but be transformed by the renewing of your mind. Then you will be able to test and approve what God's will is—His good, pleasing and perfect will."
Romans 12:2

You are beautiful!! Take a moment to dwell on this truth. What happens in your mind directly affects what happens in your life. When we shift our focus to God, He will work to transform us into what He intends for us to be by slowly changing our minds. Thoughts filled with truth, gratefulness, excellence and praise will lead you to more joy and better relationships. Of course, these changes won't happen overnight but through daily prayer and developing an intimate relationship with Christ, He can renew your mind <u>one moment</u> and <u>one thought</u> at a time, beautiful friend!

Negative thoughts don't just go away, and throughout this week we have continually been working on asking God to remove those thoughts from our minds. One way to continue to let go of these thoughts is by <u>replacing</u> them with positive thoughts. He can have power over your thoughts and your struggles with belief and time! Soon, your negative thoughts will begin to shrink as they are replaced by positive, motivating thoughts.

Say these statements out loud now:
"I am beautiful in God's eyes."
"I am in control of my nutrition."
"I am going to exercise this week."

Below, write 3 positive statements of your own that reflect the woman you want to become!

1.

2.

3.

> *"Do not be anxious about anything, but in every situation, by prayer and petition, with thanksgiving, present your requests to God."*
> *Philippians 4:6*

Transform - Give all Worry to God

Change your alarm today to Philippians 4:6 - remember this truth throughout your day. Check in with your goals and add a goal to your sheet regarding your thoughts!

Prayer

Lord, thank you for loving me unconditionally. Thank you for giving me control over my mind. Please help me to think praiseworthy thoughts as your power can transform my life.

_____
_____
_____
_____

Amen

Day Six

How are your Thoughts Being Transformed?

Spend some time in prayer, focusing on what you have learned about how powerful your mind is in regards to your whole body health. How has God been working in your heart and your mind this week to transform your thoughts? Have you experienced a newfound sense of peace and joy by shifting your thinking to positive, uplifting thoughts? Write a prayer below asking God to continue to shift your thoughts to ones of praise and excellence <u>throughout</u> the rest of your journey.

_____

_____

_____

_____

_____

_____

_____ ____

_____

_____

Day Seven

Use today to look at the exercise calendar, meal plan and your week ahead. Prepare your mind and heart for a successful, healthy week by getting organized. Tell yourself you <u>will</u> make progress this week.

Continue to take inventory of your thoughts each day, be intentional and shift them to reflect thoughts of <u>gratitude</u>!

You can transform your life one day at a time - I believe in you!

_____

_____

_____

_____

_____

Week Six

Be filled with the Spirit

ROMANS 12:2

"But the fruit of the Spirit is love, joy, peace, forbearance, kindness, goodness, faithfulness, gentleness and self-control. Against such things there is no law."
Galatians 5:22-23

Spirit

When you hear the words "filled with the Spirit" that may make you nervous. It made me nervous the first time those words jumped off the page at me. I never thought I was "holy" enough to be "filled with the Spirit" but I do know that when you ask God to be with you and pray continually you can be filled with the Spirit. Yes, He can transform your life. When the Bible talks about us being a temple, we become a temple by the Holy Spirit living in us. The Holy Spirit enables us to throw off the sin that so easily entangles us and truly live a life that God calls us to live. The only way we can truly transform from the inside out is if we allow ourselves to be filled with the Spirit of the God who loves us so much.

Memorize

".. be filled with the Spirit and live by the Spirit"
Ephesians 5:18

Reflect

What do you know about the Holy Spirit? Read Acts 2:38. The Spirit is an element to our faith that many struggle to understand, however it is vital to living a transformed life. The Spirit is who equips us to live like God calls us to live, and who gives us the strength and power to live a life that looks like Jesus'.

In John 14, Jesus tells the disciples that He "will not leave us as orphans; I will come to you." God has not left us on Earth to walk this journey alone, but He has sent someone who Jesus says "will teach us all things." Sweet friends, let's find comfort today in knowing that we are not taking this journey alone! It is God's Spirit who lives inside of us and gives us the same power that raised Jesus from the dead to live our lives for Him.

One of the first things we must do is step back and acknowledge <u>how</u> the Spirit is working in our lives so that we may allow Him to continue to work, and allow ourselves to be used by Him. Where has the Spirit been working in your life?

Once we acknowledge where the Spirit is working in our lives, we must focus on how we can allow Him to live through us in our daily lives. By sharing our faith, praying, serving others or simply sharing a kind word with someone else, you are living by the Spirit.

Galatians 5:22-23 tells us,

"But the fruit of the Spirit is love, joy, peace, patience, kindness, goodness, faithfulness, gentleness and self-control."

These are the elements that the Spirit brings forth in us when we allow Him to guide our steps and let Him truly transform our actions and our entire lives. How can you actively allow the Spirit to bear fruit through you this week?

_____

_____

_____

_____

This week we will really focus on allowing the Spirit to be very present in our lives. How can we acknowledge His presence more and allow ourselves to become more full of Him and less of ourselves?

_____

_____

_____

_____

_____

Day One

"But the fruit of the Spirit is love, joy, peace, forbearance, kindness, goodness, faithfulness, gentleness and self-control. Against such things there is no law."
Galatians 5:22-23

Sweet friend, we focused our attention last week on where we set our minds, which determines what we do and how we act. Now we will move on to learning how the Spirit is woven into our thoughts and actions. The Spirit is the means by which God accomplishes His work in us. Peter shows us in Acts 2:38 that when we repent and <u>believe</u>, we will receive the Holy Spirit in us. The Spirit is a gift given to us from God! We can not earn it. To receive the power of the Holy Spirit, we must turn from sin and ask God to change our lives!

We are told of the fruits of the Spirit in Galatians 5:22-23. Are you filled with love, joy, peace, forbearance, kindness, goodness, faithfulness, gentleness and self-control? These attributes of the Spirit are what we are striving to have more of this week in your transformation.

Which fruit(s) of the Spirit do you feel you already possess? What would you like to ask the Spirit to fill you with more of during this transformation? How can you show one of these traits of the <u>Spirit</u> today?

_____

_____

_____

_____

Life change, true transformation, comes from the power of the Holy Spirit. Let's rely on the Spirit to produce the fruits within us and transform every aspect of our lives!

"On one occasion, while he was eating with them, he gave them this command: Do not leave Jerusalem, but wait for the gift my Father promised, which you have heard me speak about. For John baptized with water, but in a few days you will be baptized with the Holy Spirit. Then they gathered around him and asked him, Lord, are you at this time going to restore the kingdom to Israel? He said to them: It is not for you to know the times or dates the Father has set by his own authority. But you will receive power when the Holy Spirit comes on you; and you will be my witnesses in Jerusalem, and in all Judea and Samaria, and to the ends of the earth." Acts 1:4-8

Read again what Christ told His disciples. How does the Scripture from the book of Acts describe how the Spirit will connect to you?

_____

_____

_____

How can you work to be filled with this power today and exemplify what a Spirit-filled life looks like to others?

_____

_____

_____

Transform - Set Goals

Add a new goal to your goal sheet describing how you can practically live a Spirit filled-life.

Rewrite your 3 main goals here.

1.

2.

3.

Prayer

Lord, thank you for giving me the gift of your Holy Spirit. Help me today to walk side by side with You as my guide. I know You desire to transform me through the power of the Holy Spirit in my life. Take control of my day and allow your Spirit to work and have your way in me, Father.

_____
_____
_____
_____

Amen

Day Two

"Those who live according to the flesh have their minds set on what the flesh desires; but those who live in accordance with the Spirit have their minds set on what the Spirit desires."
Romans 8:5

Yes, how you live your life and what you do <u>daily</u> are essential in living a transformed life. You will need ACTION and FRUIT together with TRUTH to transform your entire being. The Holy Spirit is God, and He is living inside of you! Be in prayer throughout your day with Him. Talk with him moment by moment to give Him access to every piece of your life. Ask Him to lead you and to work through you in every way possible. When we live according to the Spirit and reside in God's presence in every moment, it is then that He begins to change who we are and transform our lives so we can become more like Jesus.

How can you communicate and relate to the Holy Spirit on a daily basis?

_____

_____

_____

_____

Come to God humbly, aware of your idols and shortcomings. Through studying His Word and allowing Him to work in your life, you can access the gift of the Spirit. Do you believe that the Holy Spirit can transform your life and your health? How?

_____

_____

_____

Examples

-Prayer

-Memorizing Scripture

-Walk and talk

-Journal

-Call an encouraging friend

-Sing praises

-Quiet Times

-Church

How can you practically use the Holy Spirit to help you when you have a problem or come to a stumbling block with your transformation?

Transform - Let the Spirit Guide You

Review the Steps for Transformation on page 118 - check the boxes again and see how you can ask the Spirit to guide you in completing these steps.

Prayer

Lord, thank you for sending your Spirit to live inside of me. Bring me life and freedom today. Your power and strength can give me hope and allow me to overcome any obstacle. Holy Spirit, support me; help me in my weakness and transform my soul.

_____

_____

_____

_____

Amen

Day Three

"...Be filled with the Spirit, speaking to one another with psalms, hymns, and songs from the Spirit. Sing and make music from your heart to the Lord, always giving thanks to God the Father for everything, in the name of our Lord."
Ephesians 5:18-20

You are called to be a shining light, but is that really possible? Yes! By transforming your life one day at a time to become more like Christ, you are becoming more filled with the Spirit, shining His light to those around you. What does this look like? It is a life full of speaking, singing, thanking and praising God throughout each and every day. Slowly, we are transforming our entire body – the temple where the Holy Spirit resides. By allowing the Spirit to fill us and reside in us we can be TRANSFORMED and FILLED to the fullest measure with joy!

When we focus more on the Spirit, God allows us to see joy regardless of our situation.

Typically, we expect God to transform every aspect of our lives instantly, especially in our world of instant gratification and quick fixes. However, the Holy Spirit works in God's perfect timing, asking us and teaching us to trust Him completely, shaping and molding us into His plan slowly, one day at a time.

Have you ever wanted the Spirit to act and you felt He didn't hear you?

_____

_____

_____

How did this impact you? Can you trust the Holy Spirit now to act and help you transform your life?

_____
_____

_____

How can you work on <u>trusting</u> God's timing this week and attempt to find joy in every circumstance?

_____
_____

_____

Transform - Praise at All Times

Listen to your favorite uplifting song and spend some time praising God! <u>Share it with a friend!</u>

If you want to see the Spirit transform your life, you need to ask Him to show you. Go to Him now in prayer and ask Him to give you fruits of the Spirit and reveal to you where He is working in you.

Prayer

Compose your own prayer below

_____
_____
_____
_____
_____
_____

Amen

Day Four

"The Lord is my strength and my defense; he has become my salvation. He is my God, and I will praise him, my father's God, and I will exalt him."
Exodus 15:2

Understand - God Restores

As we spoke of rest and recovery in previous sessions, we know restoration is crucial for whole body health. God is the only one who will restore us and refresh us fully along the way. He will give us the nourishment we need to finish the race. He deeply desires for us to honor Him with our bodies so that we are available to do any good work that He has planned for us. The <u>true transformation</u> is when the Holy Spirit dwells inside of us and begins to shine brightly through every aspect of our life. Take a moment to visualize light breaking through a barrier! Beautiful one, continue to grow in love and knowledge of God <u>each</u> day. By reading God's Word, praying, and living with Him at the center we can be <u>completely</u> and <u>totally</u> transformed. Take this journey one day at a time, looking to Him to be your strength and your companion. Through His love you can grow to be more physically, emotionally and spiritually fit to love and serve in all areas of life!

Write 5 ways you seek to grow in faith one day at a time.

1.

2.

3.

4.

5.

Talk with your accountability partner today about a few of the ways you want to grow in your faith as you continue your transformation. Write about your conversation here.

_____

_____

_____

"Do not be wise in your own eyes; fear the Lord and shun evil. This will bring health to your body and nourishment to your bones." Proverbs 3:7-8

This week, encourage your partner or a friend by writing a prayer for them in a letter or note. Write below how you can continue to stay accountable with your partner after this study is over.

_____

_____

_____

_____

"Do not be wise in your own eyes; fear the Lord and shun evil. This will bring health to your body and nourishment to your bones." Proverbs 3:7-8

I will strive to encourage _____ today.

Prayer

Lord, I am so grateful for _____, my accountability partner. Give encouragement to _____ and lift her up today. Father, you are my strength and salvation. Work in my life and fill me with love, joy, peace, kindness, gentleness and self-control. Help me to live, walking in the Spirit each moment today.
Amen

Day Five

"So I say to you: <u>Ask</u> and it will be given to you; seek and you will find; knock and the door will be opened to you. For everyone who asks receives; the one who seeks finds; and to the one who knocks, the door will be opened."
Luke 11:9-10

Dear one, I have loved walking alongside you during this journey. Here is a very important question: Will you rely on your own abilities or will you allow the Spirit of Jesus Christ to use and transform you completely?

Spend extra time in prayer today, <u>asking</u> the Spirit to take what you have learned through this study and soak it into your soul- leaving you truly transformed in your body, mind and spirit. In the Holy Spirit there is truth- the answer to your issue, the problem in your heart, the disconnect in your mind. Pray that you can live out what you have learned through fellowship with others, reading God's Word, time spent in prayer and by using the tools of nutrition and exercise. My prayer is that you would take all of these things that you have learned and use them to CHANGE YOUR LIFE!

What changes have you made in your life the past 6 weeks?

1.

2.

3.

4.

5.

What changes do you want to continue to make to transform your body, mind and spirit?

1.

2.

3.

4.

5.

Make prayer an integral part of your day. Make exercise a form of worship. Sing praises out loud. Nourish your body with clean foods.

Understand- God Must be the Center

If you genuinely want to strengthen your faith, you need to <u>ask</u> God to be the center of your life each day and take action in your goals and dreams.

Prayer

Heavenly Father, I realize if I walk in step with you I can live my best life. Please become the center of my life today and transform each area of my life that needs your love. God, overwhelm me with your Spirit, show me the truth and work through me each and every day.

_____
_____
_____

Amen

Day Six

"For God so loved the world that He gave His one and only Son, that whoever believes in Him shall not perish but have eternal life."
John 3:16

Pray this verse and remind yourself today and every day of what God has done so that you can live for Him each and every day. Pray that this gospel will totally transform you to His likeness so that you can seek to live out His will and purpose for your life.

Day Seven

Beautiful sister, thank you for allowing me to walk with you for the past six weeks through your total transformational journey.

Use today to review your notes and highlight and star areas of your book that you want to continue to focus on in the next few weeks. Review the goals you set at the start of the study and see all that you have accomplished. Remember we are striving for progress, not perfection. Be proud of your progress. Talk with your accountability partner and celebrate every victory and discuss how you can continue to hold each other accountable moving forward. Allow God to be your true companion and partner and ask Him to help you achieve your goals and trust in His perfect timing.

My prayer for each of you is that you will take this study and continue to seek to live a transformed life each and every day, walking alongside the Lord and striving to live a life for Him - body, mind and spirit.

Continuing to Live Transformed

"And so, dear sisters, I plead with you to give your bodies to God because of all He has done for you. Let them be a living and holy sacrifice—the kind He will find acceptable. This is truly the way to worship Him. Don't copy the behavior and customs of this world, but let God transform you into a new person by changing the way you think. Then you will learn to know God's will for you, which is good and pleasing and perfect."
Romans 12:1-2 (NLT)

For the past six weeks, we have studied how God can work miracles of healing and transformation in our lives no matter where we have come from or how lost we seem. We have learned that miracles and change do not happen overnight or by chance. Now is the time to fully grasp the concept that true transformation requires <u>active participation</u> and <u>complete trust</u>. The fruits of the Spirit are the qualities that God will place in your body when the Holy Spirit lives through you. <u>Who you are and your true character is the sum of your habits</u>. Now, it is your responsibility to use what you have learned to develop new healthy habits to completely transform.

Being conformed is what can happen to us when we choose to follow the ways of the world. However, when we choose to be transformed by His power and love, we choose to live a life full of God! A life full of joy, peace, patience, kindness, and deep love.

Rewrite your goals for the next 4 weeks here as you will continue to transform:

1.

2.

3.

4.

5.

5 Daily Steps to Live Transformed

1. Focus on being diligent and spending time in prayer.

2. Focus on setting goals and striving to reach them.

3. Focus on improving your nutrition to treat your body as a temple.

4. Focus on seeing exercise as a form of worship.

5. Focus your mind on things above and not of this world.

"Let us not become weary in doing good, for at the proper time we will reap a harvest of blessings if we do not give up."
Galatians 6:9

Notes

Notes

Daily Checklist

☐ Have quiet time or meditation, reading Scripture
☐ Drink 8-10 glasses of water
☐ Eat protein dense foods with every meal
☐ Eat 5-7 servings of vegetables
☐ Eat 3-4 servings of fruit
☐ Sleep a minimum of 7 hours
☐ Exercise 30 minutes
☐ Practice healthy, positive self talk
☐ Encourage a friend
☐ Follow a nutrition guide
☐ Follow an exercise plan

10 Steps for Transformation

If you want to feel your best inside and outside you need a real LIFE change!! Clean the slate and make a vow to honor your body today!

1. Start a food journal. Writing down what you eat and drink in a notebook or on your favorite fitness app is one of the keys to your success. MyFitnessPal is a free app that is awesome! Keeping a food journal can help you understand any emotional motivation you may have behind your food choices and can show you when and what you need to adjust in your nutrition plan.

2. Try strength training. Muscle tissue burns more calories to maintain itself than fat—up to 50 extra calories for each additional pound of muscle. Build the toned muscles that raise metabolism by adding weights to your workout. Try traditional weights, like dumbbells, or a body weight workout. High-intensity interval training (HIIT) is especially effective at raising metabolism. Strength train 2-3 times a week for maximum transformation.

3. Reach for fat-burning foods. Avoid the foods that pump the body with too much sugar, sodium and preservatives. Instead, nourish yourself with clean, unprocessed foods that can help your body become a lean, mean, fat-burning machine.

4. Eat high protein foods. The body needs to do a lot of extra work to digest protein. Add protein-rich foods, like salmon, lean meat, Greek yogurt and quinoa to help your body to burn more calories.

5. Spice it up. Spices can help your body by increasing metabolism. Healthy recipes containing spices like turmeric and ginger are a tasty way to boost metabolism and add a zing of flavor.

6. Eat small and eat frequently. Those long stretches between the typical three meals per day lead to hunger, and that makes the body think it's starving, which causes your metabolism to slow down. Eating four to six smaller, protein dense meals each day ensures that you're nourishing the body before it goes into starvation mode and starts storing fat.

7. Get your daily water and caffeine. Drinking at least 64 ounces of water a day (120 oz if endurance training) is so important for a healthy lifestyle. Also, caffeine, a stimulant, acts as a temporary metabolism booster, so enjoy 50-100 milligrams per day. Avoid soda and get your caffeine from unsweetened coffee or green tea.

8. Have a plan! Follow an exercise and nutrition plan. Be willing to modify the plan if needed. Listen to what your body needs and what it can handle on any given day

9. Have patience. It takes 8-12 weeks for cardio-respiratory and muscular/metabolic adaptations to occur, 8 weeks for strength and flexibility. These adaptations will continue to build progressively for years.

10. Reflect. Give yourself the much needed time to reflect daily on the important things in life. An attitude of gratitude will help your overall well being! Start a gratitude journal!

"Do you not know that your body is a temple of the Holy Spirit, who is in you, whom you have received from God? You are not your own; you were bought at a price. Therefore honor God with your body."
1 Corinthians 6: 19-20

Transformation Goals
this Month

1. _____
2. _____
3. _____

Next 6 Months

1. _____
2. _____
3. _____

Next Year

1. _____
2. _____
3. _____

Best High Protein Snacks

Protein is an essential food for repairing muscle tissues, especially after a long run or workout and protein keeps you feeling full for longer. High protein snacks should be consumed within 30-45 minutes after workouts for maximum muscle repair and building benefits, or should be consumed as a snack during the day to fight cravings and help manage weight. Women should try to get between 15-25 grams of protein after a workout or run. Below are some great snacks that are high in protein, many of which can be eaten on the go during a busy day.

1/4 cup of almonds- 10g
1 cheese stick- 8g
4 oz of low fat cottage cheese- 14g
1 hard boiled egg- 6g
1 cup fat free Greek yogurt- 20g
1 cup cooked Edamame- 17g
2 slices of turkey breast deli meat- 8g
1 cup soy milk- 8g
1/2 cup chickpeas- 18g
1/2 cup black beans- 20g
1/2 cup cashews- 10g
1/2 cup sunflower seeds- 12g
3 oz of tuna- 25g
2 tbsp of peanut butter- 8g
Protein Shake- 15-25g

Mix up how you combine the different snacks to add variety to your day. Try trail mix with a few different types of nuts or add fresh fruit into your Greek yogurt. Varying your nutrients daily is beneficial in allowing your body to transform.

Getting Started Guide

☐ Clean out pantry and refrigerator
☐ Reduce highly processed items (Chips, white bread, white pasta, sugary cereals, sugary snacks like doughnuts, sugary yogurts, processed pre-made items, margarine)
☐ Make snack baskets
☐ Fill with Kind bars, Luna bars, trail mix (homemade or store bought with low sugar content) LARA bars, nuts, rice cakes, popcorn, low sugar granola)
☐ Tupperware Inventory
☐ Have tupperware ready for pre-making salads and other food prep for the week.
☐ Large water pitcher (goal is to have a minimum of 64 oz water per day)
☐ Fruit bowls for counter tops
☐ Fill with apples, bananas, plums, etc to grab when feeling hungry. Make snacking easy and healthy!
☐ Snack-sized plastic bags (best for portion control)
☐ Measuring cups and spoons (food scale is an incredibly helpful tool as well)
☐ Super-foods stocked
    ☐ Lean red meat (grass-fed preferred)
    ☐ Salmon (wild caught preferred)
    ☐ Eggs (Omega-3 and cage-free preferred)
    ☐ Plain Greek yogurt
    ☐ Protein supplements (whey, milk or plant protein sources)
    ☐ Spinach, Cruciferous vegetables (broccoli, cabbage, cauliflower)
    ☐ Mixed berries
    ☐ Whole oats
    ☐ Raw, unsalted mixed nuts
    ☐ Avocados

☐ Olive oil (extra virgin preferred)
☐ Fish oil
☐ Flax seeds (ground)
☐ Chia seeds
☐ Green tea
☐ Kale

Tips

- Read all ingredients - if food is filled with chemicals and words that you aren't familiar with, you probably don't want it entering your amazing body!
- Aim for cage-free eggs, grass-fed beef, natural organic chicken
- Try unsweetened almond, coconut or cashew milk for cereal and coffee
- Use extra virgin olive oil as your main oil and base for salad dressings
- Try cutting out excess enriched bread, and cut out most white breads, pastas, potatoes, etc.
- Look for a quality protein powder that can be used in many recipes as well as smoothies! Favorite: Raw Fit Vanilla or Vega.

Total Transformation Strength Workout

BUTT KICK RUNS-IN PLACE
1 min

FORWARD LUNGES WITH LATERAL SHOULDER RAISE
10 each leg

SLOW MOUNTAIN CLIMBERS
15 each leg

TRICEP DIPS
15-20 reps

DEAD-LIFT WITH BICEP CURL
15 reps

FULL SQUAT WITH SHOULDER PRESS
15 reps

FRONT BOXER KICKS
20 reps

MINI PLANK LEG LIFTS
15 each leg

REVERSE LUNGES HOLDING WEIGHTS
10 each leg

FULL WIDE ARM PUSH-UPS
15 all out

REPEAT 3x! Stretch 5 min

Transformational Bodyweight Workout

GRAPEVINES, JUMP ROPE, JOG IN PLACE
1 min each

SUMO SQUATS
25 each

BICYCLE CRUNCHES
40 reps

REVERSE PLANK & HOLD
30 sec x 2

YOGA/CHATTARANGA PUSH-UPS
15 reps

CURTSY LUNGES
15 each leg

MINI SIDE PLANK (ELBOWS) & HOLD EACH SIDE
30 sec x 2

REVERSE LUNGES
15 each leg

FULL PLANK ALTERNATE KNEES INTO CHEST
15 each leg

JUMPING JACKS
1 min

REPEAT 2x! Stretch 5 min

Transformational HIIT Workout

Set interval timer for 45 sec interval 15 sec rest

POWER JACKS

LUNGE JUMPS OR ALTERNATING FORWARD LUNGES
(Lightly)

SPIDERMAN
(Full plank, alternate - knee comes to outside touching elbow)

REVERSE PLANK & HOLD-ALTERNATE STRAIGHT LEG LIFTS
(Straight arms & legs)

JOG IN PLACE
(High knees)

WIDE-ARM PUSH-UPS
(Stay strong in your core, no arch in your back)

SIDE LUNGES

TRICEP DIPS IN BRIDGE POSITION

SQUAT JUMPS
(Explode into the air)

MINI SIDE PLANK W/ HIP LIFTS

REPEAT 3x! Stretch 5 min

Transformational Beginner's Workout
(Light weights or no weights used)

WALK IN PLACE
1 min

SLOW SQUATS
10-12 reps

BALANCE ON ONE LEG, BICEP CURLS
8 curls on each leg

STANDING SIT-UPS
20 reps

FULL PLANK & HOLD
30 sec x 2

CALF RAISES
15 reps

TRICEP EXTENSION
(Using one weight) 12 reps

FULL PLANK ALTERNATE KNEES INTO CHEST
10 each leg

SIDE LATERAL SHOULDER RAISE
12 reps

REPEAT 2x! Stretch 5 min

Transformational Arms and Abs Workout

(Dumbbells needed)

15 SQUAT WITH SHOULDER PRESS

30 SECOND FULL PLANK

15 BICEP CURL WITH FORWARD LUNGE

30 SECOND PLANK ALTERNATE KNEES IN

15 TRICEP EXTENSION

30 SECOND PRONE PLANK

15 LATERAL SHOULDER RAISE

30 SECOND FULL PLANK WITH LEG LIFTS

15 FULL PUSH-UPS

JUMP ROPE 1 MINUTE

REPEAT 3X! Stretch 5 min

Romans 12:2

Special thanks to my loving family who has supported me through this journey. I appreciate all the amazing comments and feedback from friends and family. I have grown so much through writing this study and my prayer is that you can take away many pieces to complete your journey and help you LIVE transformed!

Please email me at transfitathens@gmail.com with any feedback or comments!

Blessings,

Caroline

transFit
body · mind · spirit
www.transitathens.com

	Breakfast	AM Snack	Lunch	PM Snack	Dinner	Exercise
S PREP DAY!	Easy Egg Muffins, 2 slices nitrate-free turkey bacon, 1/2 cup raspberries/ blueberries	1 sliced pear sprinkled with cinnamon 1/4 cup unsalted nuts	FREE MEAL or Clean out the fridge & fix a large salad with leftover veggies! PREP: Salads, Overnight Oats, chop veggies/fruit	1/3 cup edamame 1 cutie cup green tea	Delicious Maple Dijon Chicken, cup Roasted Brussels Sprouts, cup Cauliflower Bites	Rest Day! Or 30 minutes Yoga
M	Super Green Protein Smoothie	1 hard-boiled egg 1 apple	Chicken Salad with Grapes over bed of spinach cup of carrot sticks	1 cup cucumbers or carrot sticks with 2 Tbsp. cottage cheese or hummus cup green tea	Slow Cooker Pork Tenderloin Fajitas with all the fixings! Lettuce wrap for you, tortilla for family!	Strength Training 55 minutes
T	Easy Egg Muffins, 2 slices nitrate-free turkey bacon, 1/2 cup raspberries/ blueberries	Kind Bar	Leftover Fajitas in a bowl or lettuce wrap	Chobani 100-calorie yogurt with 1 Tbsp. unsweetened coconut flakes, 1/2 cup berries cup green tea	Turkey Meatballs with spaghetti squash or zucchini noodles (WW) angel hair pasta for family)	Steady Cardio 60 minutes
W	Overnight Oats	1 sliced pear sprinkled with cinnamon 1/4 cup unsalted nuts	Spinach Salad with Blueberries & Pecans	1 cup cucumbers or carrot sticks with 2 Tbsp. cottage cheese or hummus cup green tea	FREE MEAL/LEFTOVERS Preferably lean protein with a green veggie!	Body Weight Workout 55 minutes
T	Super Green Protein Smoothie	Kind Bar	FREE MEAL Practice making wise choices!	Chobani 100-calorie yogurt with 1 Tbsp. unsweetened coconut flakes, 1/2 cup berries cup green tea	Orange Marmalade Glazed Salmon, cup Oven Roasted Asparagus, 1/4 cup quinoa	Cardio Intervals 60 minutes
F	Overnight Oats	1 hard-boiled egg 1 apple	Chicken Salad with Grapes over bed of spinach cup of carrot sticks	1/3 cup edamame 1 cutie cup green tea	Date Night/FREE MEAL Remember: grilled, baked, steamed or broiled!!	Strength Training 55 minutes
S	2 fried eggs using 1 tsp. coconut oil, 1/2 avocado sliced & sprinkled with hemp seeds, 1/2 cup berries	1 sliced pear sprinkled with cinnamon 1/4 cup unsalted nuts	Spinach Salad with Blueberries & Pecans	1 cup cucumbers or carrot sticks with 2 Tbsp. cottage cheese or hummus cup green tea	Fire up the grill! 1 Grass Fed Burger, cup sweet potato fries, small side salad cup frozen berries for treat!	Power Walk or Run 4 miles or 60 minutes

Made in the USA
Columbia, SC
04 December 2022

72680286R00077